Beer
Trivia

Also by the author

American Breweries,
with Manfred Friedrich and Robert Gottschalk

The Handbook of Beer Advertising Openers
and Corkscrews: An Alphabetical Composite,
with Edward R. Kaye

A Price Guide to Beer Advertising Openers
and Corkscrews

Beer Advertising Openers: A Pictorial Guide

The Register of United States Breweries,
with Manfred Friedrich

The Register of United States Breweries:
Volume II—An Alphabetical Index,
with Manfred Friedrich

Beer Trivia

500 Questions and Answers About the World's Most Popular Drink

Donald Bull

BEAUFORT BOOKS Publishers • NEW YORK

Library of Congress Cataloging in Publication Data

Bull, Donald.
Beer trivia.

1. Beer—Miscellanea.   I. Title.
TP577.B86   1985   641.2′3   85-7492
ISBN 0-8253-0317-6

Published in the United States by Beaufort Books Publishers, New York.

Designer: Christine Swirnoff / Libra Graphics, Inc.

Printed in the U.S.A.   First Edition

10   9   8   7   6   5   4   3   2   1

Contents

Contents

Once Upon
a Time...

Once upon a time . . .

1. When was the first beer brewed in America?

2. Did Noah carry beer in his cargo on the Ark?

3. Who published a paper called "Studies on Beer" in 1876 that was a study of beer fermentation?

4. Who wrote about beer, "I wish to see this beverage become common instead of the whiskey which kills one third of our citizens and ruins their families"?

5. The first Masonic Lodge met in what Lexington, Massachusetts, tavern in 1797?

6. Which amendment repealed the Prohibition amendment?

7. Who was King Gambrinus?

8. What happened on January 24, 1935, to change the brewing industry?

9. A cannonball from the Battle of Ridgefield (April 17, 1777) is still embedded in the wall of what Ridgefield, Connecticut tavern?

10. What English tavern was frequented by authors William Shakespeare, Ben Jonson, and Christopher Marlowe?

11. At what time and date did national Prohibition go into effect?

12. At what Lexington, Massachusetts, tavern did the Minutemen assemble to await the arrival of the British on April 19, 1775?

13. What did Rheingold Brewing Company employees do in 1973 to demonstrate the brewery's serious economic problems to city and labor leaders?

14. Which amendment to the Constitution set national Prohibition in motion?

15. What was the "noble experiment"?

16. When was the American Temperance Society formed?

17. What was the name of the tavern from which the Pilgrims departed in Chaucer's *Canterbury Tales*?

18. What significant change took place in the beer can in 1960?

19. In what year was the Prohibition amendment repealed?

20. When did the German beer drinking festival Oktoberfest begin?

21. In what year was the national Prohibition amendment ratified?

22. What was the name of the bill passed in March, 1933, allowing the sale of 3.2 beer?

23. Which state adopted the first container deposit law?

24. What were Pablo, Famo, Vivo, Lux-O, and Bevo?

25. Who did a hatchet job on the Carey Hotel in Wichita, Kansas, in 1900?

26. What did Robert Smith of Dresden, Germany, invent in 1892?

27. What did Poughkeepsie, New York, brewer Matthew Vassar start in 1865?

28. When and where was the Prohibition Party organized?

29. What event destroyed the Doyle, Huck, Jerusalem, Lill & Diversey, Metz, Mueler, Sands, and Schmidt breweries?

30. What antidrinking group was formed in Boston in 1826?

Making Beer

Making beer

31. What term is used for beer that has been fermented but needs to be cooled and stored for aging?

32. What purpose does yeast serve in the brewing process?

33. How many gallons of beer are in a full barrel of beer?

34. What product introduces fermentation in the brewing process?

35. What type of beer was named after the city Pilsen in Czechoslovakia?

36. What were the five beer ingredients required by the Purity Laws set forth by the Dukes of Bavaria in 1487?

37. What is the branch of chemistry dealing with fermentation?

38. Which ingredient forms the palest beer—barley, corn, rice, or wheat?

39. What is ale?

40. How many ounces in a barrel of beer?

41. What product is used to force beer from kegs?

42. What is malt liquid called before it reaches the fermenting stage?

43. What type of plant are hops?

44. What is a germinated grain used in the brewing process?

45. What are the dried ripe cones of the flowers of a twining dioecious plant used in brewing?

46. What is a dark, sweet brew made of roasted malt and hops?

Why does it taste like this?

47. What beer is known as "pale stale ale, the beer with the foam on the bottom"?

48. What beer was advertised as "Diamond clear" and "From perfect brewing water"?

49. What brewery advertised its beer as "smooth mellow beer"?

50. What Ohio brewer advertised its Ben Brew as "100% grain"?

51. What beer was advertised as having "age-strength-purity"?

52. What beer's advertisements called it "Bonded beer" and "Plainly age-dated"?

53. What Ohio brewery said it produced Nick Thomas Beer "for goodness sake"?

54. What Delphos, Ohio, beer was claimed to be "Always fresh"?

55. Gozo, advertised as "The most delicious cereal beverage," was produced by what St. Joseph, Missouri, brewery during Prohibition?

56. "It's mellow" described what Davenport, Iowa, beer?

57. What Colorado brewery produced what they called "Triple brewed beer & ale"?

58. What beer was proclaimed to be "always the same"?

59. Name "The beer with a snap to it."

60. "B'Gosh, it's good" was a slogan for which Wisconsin beer?

61. What beer was dubbed "A Truly Fine Pale Beer"?

62. What brewery described its brand Topaz as "A Gem of Purity" and "Good to the Last Drop"?

The Brewers

The brewers

63. What Michigan brewer produced Big Mac beer from 1955–1960 in honor of the bridge spanning the strait between Michigan's upper and lower peninsulas?

64. A toy silver top is pictured on Silver Top brand beer cans. What brewery produced this beer?

65. The John F. Kennedy Center for the Performing Arts was built on the site of which old brewery?

66. Name America's oldest operating brewery.

67. What Detroit brewery survived national Prohibition by going into the production of ice cream, soft drinks, near beer, and malt extract?

68. White Motor Corporation of Canada built ten Streamliner tractors in 1947 for what Canadian brewery?

69. Which brewery took over sponsorship of the Los Angeles Dodgers in 1984 after seven years of sponsorship by Anheuser-Busch?

70. In which brewery were scenes for the 1983 movie *Strange Brew* shot?

71. Which brewery introduced the sixteen ounce can?

72. Which Brooklyn, New York, brewery sponsored beauty contests as part of its advertising campaign in the forties and fifties?

73. What brewery received a medal for purity at the 1900 Paris Exposition and a gold medal at the 1904 St. Louis World's Fair for its Peerless Beer?

74. What brewery was established in 1900 and used "Taste & Cheer" as part of its advertising slogan?

75. "My Favorite" was used as a slogan by which brewery?

76. Which brewery had the San Francisco phone number SU-0120?

77. Which large brewery is owned by a cigarette manufacturer?

78. What two brewing giants were founded by the same brewing family in Milwaukee?

79. Which brewery is recognized by the principal trademarks the Nightwalker and the Professor?

80. What two breweries were sites for the filming of the movie *Take This Job and Shove It*?

81. What brewery produced the brands Sunset, Sunset Bud, Noch-eins, Imperial, and Salvator prior to Prohibition?

82. What brewery had its origins in a former automobile factory in Cleveland, Ohio?

83. With what two cartoon characters and with which brewery are the cartoon characters Countess and Office Suds associated?

84. What brewing firm operates a porcelain factory?

85. Although the setting of the movie *F.I.S.T.* was Cleveland, Ohio, some of the bar scenes were filmed in the hospitality room in this brewery.

86. Anheuser-Busch sued this Pennsylvania brewer for infringing upon their Budweiser name.

87. What brewery issued a series of fourteen cans called the Tooner Schooners that featured words from famous songs?

88. What brewery produced 500 Ale for distribution at the Indianapolis 500 races?

89. What was the first brewery to nationally market beer in lift-tab top cans?

90. What was the first major national brewery to can beer?

91. What Crete, Nebraska, brewery produced Golden Harvest Beer?

92. What St. Paul, Minnesota, brewery aged its beer in caves?

93. What brewery produced Pink Elephant Ale?

94. The "Brew that satisfies" was produced by what New York brewer?

95. What Chicago brewer produced Magnet Beer?

96. Nine Months Old Perfection beer was produced by what brewer?

What's your pleasure?

97. Name a beer brand from the Arizona Brewing Company of Phoenix, Arizona, that featured an Indian in its advertising.

98. What popular Canadian beer brand name was also used by San Francisco's General Brewing Company?

99. Maier Brewing Company of Los Angeles, California, produced L & M Beer from 1956–1969. What did *L* and *M* stand for?

100. What beer was associated with the Portland, Oregon, radio station KGON on 92.3 F.M.?

101. What beer sponsored the 1984 American Motorcycle Association Motocross National Championship in Mt. Morris, Pennsylvania?

102. What soft drink did the Lone Star Brewing Company of San Antonio, Texas, begin producing in the shadow of the oncoming Prohibition?

103. Name the low-calorie drink introduced by Anheuser-Busch in 1978 that was a blend of lemon, lime, ginger, and apple.

104. Hudepohl and Schmidt brewing companies introduced the first low-alcohol beers. What were they called?

105. In April 1983 this controversial beer was introduced to the Los Angeles market.

106. August Busch introduced this beverage in 1916 as a measure to keep his business thriving should national Prohibition pass.

107. What was the official beer of the 1982 Knoxville, Tennessee, World's Fair?

108. What brand name used by the Louis Obert Brewing Company of St. Louis and later the Beth Uhl Brewing Company of Bethlehem, Pennsylvania, was taken from the name of an opera by Richard Wagner?

109. What beer did Burt Reynolds drink while canoeing in the movie *Deliverance*?

110. What do the brewers Falls City, West End, Cold Spring, and Pearl have in common?

111. What do cans of Primo Beer, Schlitz Malt Liquor, and Gluek Stite Beer have in common?

112. What beer did the Sunshine Brewing Company of Reading, Pennsylvania, produce and later curtail when threatened by a lawsuit from Hugh Hefner's Playboy empire?

113. What beer was named after a famous fictional spy?

114. From 1957–1962 Fox Head Brewing Company of Waukesha, Wisconsin, brewed this brand "For Men Only."

115. What was the name of the beer made by the West Bend Lithia Company of West Bend, Wisconsin, that was marketed to the black population?

116. What beer brand did Maier Brewing Company distribute in limited quantity in Los Angeles and that was associated with the Watts riots of the sixties?

117. Name two beers with space-age names.

118. This beer was advertised as "Colorado's light refreshing beer," "Mountain high in quality," and "Tastes better, costs less."

119. What beer brand sports a blue ribbon on its product containers?

120. What was the first beer brand to appear in cans?

121. What beer is known as the "Champagne of Beers"?

122. "That's the Beer" was a slogan for what brand of what brewery?

123. What St. Louis beer is associated with the slogan "Choicest Product of the Brewer's Art"?

Trademarks

Trademarks

124. What character was the advertising symbol for Marathon City Brewing Company, Marathon, Wisconsin?

125. A pretty girl riding high in the sky on a quarter moon is used in what beer advertising campaign?

126. The scene of a black whale rising from the sea was used in the advertising of what beer?

127. What was the elderly, bearded figure in Bartels Brewing Company advertising called?

128. When did the A & Eagle trademark of Anheuser-Busch first appear?

129. A knight in armor was the trademark of this Jeannette, Pennsylvania, brewer.

130. What kind of musician was featured in advertising of Bosch Brewing Company of Houghton, Michigan?

131. What Philadelphia brewery had a man riding a high-wheeler bicycle as its symbol?

132. What was the Bartels Brewing Company trademark of a Viking holding a stein and an axe called?

133. The Ballantine beer trademark is made up of three rings. What words appear on the rings?

134. What do the A and Eagle in the Anheuser-Busch trademark symbolize?

135. What brewery made the K Man waiter famous?

136. What Buffalo, New York, brewery used the head of a Native American as its trademark?

137. A man in a top hat appeared in this upstate New York brewer's advertising. What product was advertised and by whom?

138. What type of person was featured in Jones Brewing Company advertising for Stoney's beer?

139. What New York brewer used an elf in its advertising?

140. What Ohio brewer used a wooden shoe as its trademark?

141. What Milwaukee brewer was identified by a globe of the world?

Who's Who?

Who's who?

142. He did a television commercial urging Philadelphians to try Joe's Beer.

143. What beer did Judge Roy Bean sell in his Jersey Lilly Tavern in Langtry, Texas?

144. Bob Elliott and Ray Goulding were the voices for two sets of characters in commercials. What characters did they play for what breweries?

145. For what beer did Joe Namath do television ads?

146. What actor was a spokesperson in 1950s magazine advertising for Blatz Beer?

147. This former New York Yankee announcer called home runs Ballantine Blasts during the fifties.

148. Joe Edwards of St. Louis introduced Rock & Roll Beer in 1984. What music legend appeared on the first can of Rock & Roll Beer?

149. Who did the voices of West End Brewing Company's Schultz and Dooley in the 1950s and 1960s advertising campaign?

150. What do the brewing names Busch, Pabst, and Gettelman have in common?

151. What St. Louis brewer had an interest in a San Antonio, Texas, brewery?

152. Who said, "Persons intoxicated with wine pass out lying on their faces, while those drunk with beer invariably lie on their backs"?

153. Harpo Marx appeared in the advertising campaign of which Canadian brewer?

154. Who played the mad brewmaster of the Elsinore Brewery in the 1983 movie *Strange Brew*?

155. Who was the first Miss Rheingold?

156. In commercials he said, "My family name is on the label. And to me beer is thicker than water," and "You may not like my mug, but you'll love my beer."

157. What comic strip character can be found in the local pubs with his wife Florrie when not at home arguing with her about his excessive beer consumption?

158. Who wrote, "For a quart of ale is a dish fit for a King"?

159. Who said, "No beer less than five months old will ever be sold out of this brewery"?

160. Who said, "For me the beer thing was a natural, 'cause I know a good beer better than anybody. Who knows? Maybe I'll become the Colonel Sanders of beer"?

161. August Krug founded a brewery in Milwaukee in 1849 that became a major brewing concern under the name of the individual who married his widow. Who became Krug's widow's new husband in 1856?

162. What is Homer Conner of South Carolina using to build a twenty-two foot sailboat in his yard?

163. In what movie can Burt Reynolds be seen drinking a can of Lucky Lager Beer?

164. Who played Charlie Pickett in the movie *Take This Job and Shove It* filmed at Pickett's brewery in Dubuque, Iowa?

165. In conjunction with beer, what did Alexander Hamilton, John Hancock, Patrick Henry, and James Madison have in common?

166. Who appeared in commercials stating, "If there's one thing I like better than telling people what goes into my beer, it's meeting the people my beer goes into"?

167. Dave Thomas and Rick Moranis played the McKenzie Brothers in this brewery spoof movie.

168. What famous mobster was associated with the beer brands Canadian Ace, Manhattan Premium, and All Star?

169. What early American brewed beer at Monticello?

170. Howard Hughes was one of the money men behind what Texas brewery?

171. Dutch artist Franz Hals was the inspiration for can designs for Hals Beer. What brewery produced Hals Beer?

172. What early American brewed beer at Mount Vernon?

173. Which of the 1957 Miss Rheingolds went on to become a movie star?

174. What did Ermal C. Fraze of the Dayton Reliable Tool Company of Dayton, Ohio, invent?

175. Name a famous Revolutionary War general who operated a tavern in Brooklyn, New York, before joining the war effort.

176. For what did Thomas Kensett and Ezra Daggett receive a patent in 1825?

177. What was expected to happen when a Galveston, Texas, carpenter said, "They said today that we should stock up on canned goods. So I went out and bought a case of beer"?

178. Whose picture appeared in advertising of the English Mansfield Brewery Company with the copy "He might be president of the most powerful nation on earth, but he's never had a pint of Mansfield"?

179. What does a cooper make?

180. Which organization was Carrie Nation associated with?

181. Who invented the bottle (crown) cap?

182. What United States senator was known as the "enforcer" of Prohibition?

183. Who brewed the first lager beer in America?

184. What ex-football coach starred in Miller Lite television commercials?

185. What actor starred in Schlitz Light television commercials?

Places

Places

186. In what year and where was Pabst awarded its blue ribbon?

187. What type of plant operated in the Lone Star brewhouse from 1921–1925 (the early years of Prohibition)?

188. What is the significance of Mathaser Hall in Munich, Germany?

189. What tavern was the site of George Washington's farewell address to the Continental Army as well as where the United States State Department was founded?

190. What is at the top of the steeple of the First Baptist Church of Hampton Falls, New Hampshire?

191. Where are the beers Dreher, Peroni, Raffo, Moretti, and Paretti brewed?

192. What was the name of the hospitality room at the Schlitz brewery in Milwaukee?

193. At what brewery was the movie *Take This Job and Shove It* filmed?

194. Where might you hear "When you're out of Point, you're out of town"?

195. This Chicago restaurant offers its own brand of beer during its festivals celebrating bock beer, May wine, Old Heidelberg, and Christmas.

196. What was the name of the bar frequented by the working class in the movie *F.I.S.T.*?

197. In what Virginia tavern did the House of-Burgesses meet in 1774 to voice their support for blockades in Boston?

198. Tiger beer was named after what college's football team?

199. Name seven states for which there were no breweries with the same name as the state.

200. In what city was Al Capone's Manhattan Brewing Company located?

201. In what city was the beer tray conceived?

202. Where was the Mile High Brewery located?

203. Where was the Auto City Brewing Company located?

204. Which state has never had a brewery?

Do You Know?

Do you know?

205. What is *biru*?

206. What is a conner?

207. Name a very strong ale produced for British troops serving in India in the nineteenth century.

208. A white colored, yeasty beer traditionally served in a wide-bowled stem glass with a bit of raspberry syrup.

209. What is *cerveza*?

210. What term is applied to an English pub or inn that has contracted to buy all its beer from a single brewer?

211. What are downrights and block hooks?

212. What matrimonial term comes from an eleventh century English custom?

213. What is a growler?

214. What do the German beer terms *helles* and *dunkels* mean?

215. What is the French word for beer?

216. What term was applied to women who operated British alehouses in the sixteenth and seventeenth centuries?

217. What is a Czechoslovakian boot glass used in beer drinking contests called?

218. What are Asahi, Kirin, Sapporo, and Suntory?

219. What line of pottery did Coors Brewery, a subsidiary of Coors Porcelain Company, introduce in the 1940s?

220. How many bottles of "beer on the wall" are there in the song?

221. What was the name of Rudy Schaefer's (Schaefer Brewing Company) yacht?

222. What word runs vertically on the side of Anheuser-Busch's Budweiser label?

223. What is a ring pull?

224. What term is applied to a person favoring the sale of alcoholic beverages?

225. What is the German word for beer?

226. What type of beer is drawn from a cask or keg?

227. What is an earthenware mug for beer called?

228. What is the name for a tall glass for beer that is tapered at the bottom?

229. What term is applied to a building where beer is made?

230. What is mead?

231. What is a *brasserie*?

232. What is a hogshead?

233. What do the letters *I.R.T.P.* on beer cans produced prior to March, 1950 mean?

234. What is draft beer?

235. What term is applied to a person favoring Prohibition?

236. What term is applied to beer advertising collectibles?

237. What was a beer comb used for?

238. What is the origin of the word *beer*?

239. What does the German word *Lager* mean?

240. What popular expression is associated with pints and quarts of beer served in taverns?

Animals

Animals

241. What animal is on the weathervane in Sterling Brewing Company (Evansville, Indiana) advertising?

242. What animal is depicted in James Hanley Brewing Company (Providence, Rhode Island) advertising?

243. What animal was used by the Pointer Brewing Company of Clinton, Iowa, in its advertising?

244. What animal was featured in the Duquesne Brewing Company (Pennsylvania) advertising for Old Nut Brown Ale?

245. What famous race horses appeared in a Miller Lite Commercial?

246. What animal appears on most Bock beer bottle labels?

247. What animal was depicted on the labels of the Anheuser-Busch beverage Bevo?

248. What cartoon character of the 1950s and 1960s did Olympia Brewing Company resurrect in 1978?

249. With what beer is the armadillo associated?

250. What was Brewster the Goebel Booster?

251. What animal is pictured on Schlitz Malt Liquor cans?

252. What animal appears on the cans of August Schell Brewing Company of New Ulm, Minnesota?

253. What Cranston, Rhode Island, brewer produced canned beer called Williams Purple Cow?

254. Buffalo Brewing of Sacramento, California; Southern Brewing of Los Angeles, California; and Blitz-Weinhard of Portland, Oregon all named a beer after what animal?

255. What bird is on the cans of Sebewaing Brewing Company of Sebewaing, Michigan?

256. What animal appears on the cans of the Manhattan Brewing Company of Chicago and the Jackson Brewing Company of New Orleans?

257. A malt liquor from Pittsburgh Brewing Company has what animal on the can?

The Numbers Game

The numbers game

258. Where was One-Two Beer brewed?

259. Name two brewers who used the number forty-five in their brand name.

260. What Cincinnati brewer produced Chevy 85 Ale?

261. What was the number that Ziegler Brewing Company of Beaver Dam, Wisconsin, used as a name for one of its beers?

262. Stallion XII Brand Malt Liquor was produced by what brewer?

263. Who made Royal 58 Beer?

264. Who made Parkside 50 Beer?

265. What Louisville, Kentucky, brewer used the number 92 in its brand name?

266. What brewer produced Old 39 Ale?

267. What brewer produced Old 99 Ale?

268. What brewer produced Old 93 Beer?

269. What brand was sold by Tennessee Brewing Company of Memphis; Queen City Brewing of Cumberland, Maryland; and Atlantic (Lederer) Brewing Company of Chicago?

270. What number is found on cans of Fox Head beer from Waukesha, Wisconsin?

271. 1884 Beer and Ale were produced by what Ohio brewer?

272. 1884 Golden Ale was produced by what Ohio brewer?

273. 1896 Ale was produced by what Massachusetts brewer?

274. What Philadelphia brewer produced 1880 Beer?

275. What New Jersey brewer produced 1859 Beer?

276. What brewery produced 9 Horse Ale from 1933–1935, and 12 Horse Ale from 1933–1964?

277. Name two affiliated brewers who used the figure $1,000 in their brand names.

278. The Oconto Brewing Company of Oconto, Wisconsin, said of this beer, which was produced under the Fox Brewing Company label of Oconto, "Bright as Gold." What was the beer?

279. Their 500 Ale cans picture racing cars. Name the brewer.

280. Who made Private Stock 22 Beer?

Canned Beer

Canned beer

281. Which brewery produced Golden Gate Beer, which featured a picture of the Golden Gate Bridge on the can?

282. For what event did Carling Brewing Company put out a commemorative can on June 4, 1957?

283. Name six brewers who pictured a bulldog on their "Bull Dog" malt liquor cans.

284. What can company worked with Pittsburgh Brewing Company to bring out the first lift tab can in 1962?

285. What brewery's product appeared in the cans of the first beer canned in Canada?

286. What Louisville, Kentucky—home of the Kentucky Derby—brewer produced a beer can with a picture of a horse race on it?

287. Since playing cards and beer go together, Dawson decided to put a card on its Dawson's Pale Ale can (New Bedford, Massachusetts). Can you name it?

288. A steamboat appeared on this Evansville, Indiana, beer can. What was the brewer and the brand?

289. What Boston brewery featured a lighthouse on its canned beer?

290. What Albany, New York, brewer featured a shamrock on its beer cans?

291. What Burlington, Wisconsin, beer can featured a Dutch girl and windmill?

292. What did Anheuser-Busch's Budweiser Beer and Wiedemann Brewing Company's Bohemian Special have in common?

293. For several years Rheingold Breweries of New York sponsored the Miss Rheingold contests. Miss Rheingold appeared on the Rheingold beer can in only one year. What year was it?

294. What brewery issued the G. B. Fleet Car can series featuring drawings of sports cars?

295. What brewery issued cans with Parti-Quiz questions on them in the late 1950s?

296. What hockey team did Carling Black Label honor on its beer can?

297. What Detroit beer cans of the 1950s listed sports facts?

298. This Indiana brewery ran a horoscope series on its cans.

299. What beer cans showed cartoon portraits of "royalty" with the line "Beer With Us"?

300. What brand of beer was first used in Pittsburgh Brewing Company's introduction of the lift tab can with the "New easy open snap top" promotion?

301. G. Krueger Company of Newark, New Jersey, introduced the first beer in cans in 1935. What did they introduce in 1941?

302. What company developed the Conoweld process of welding can seams?

303. What company developed the Mira Seam can?

304. National Brewing Company of Phoenix, Arizona, canned this beer in the 1970s and put Phoenix Suns Basketball schedules on the cans. Name the beer.

305. What can company produced cans under the trade names Keglet and Kan Keg?

306. What was the trade name for Continental Can Company's first cans?

307. What was the trade name for Crown, Cork & Seal Company's first cans?

308. What was the trade name for American Can Company's first can?

309. What is a camouflage can?

310. What can manufacturer produced the first cone top cans?

311. What do Old Ranger and Bull's Eye beer cans have in common?

312. What brand of beer was the first beer to be packaged and sold in cans?

313. When was canned beer introduced?

314. What do Lee Remick, Dudley Moore, and Donald Duck have in common with the beer can?

315. What kind of shoe is pictured on cans of Olympia Beer, Colt 45 Malt Liquor, and Thorobred Malt Liquor?

316. What kind of vehicle was pictured on Grace Brothers Clipper Pale Beer can?

317. What is pictured on cans of Tahoe Pale Dry Beer (Grace Brothers, Santa Rosa, California); Ruser Lager Beer (Arizona Brewing Company, Phoenix, Arizona); and Kodiak Cream Ale (Schmidt Brewing, Philadelphia, Pennsylvania)?

318. What brewery was the first to introduce beer in cone top cans?

319. What brewery introduced the lift tab can?

Fit for a king

320. This Pennsylvania brewery advertised their Royal Brew as "Fit for a king."

321. This Brooklyn brewery also proclaimed its beer "Fit for a King."

322. Name a Detroit beer with the slogan "King of beers."

323. What nationally marketed beer is called the "King of Beers"?

324. The Chief Beer was produced by what Minnesota brewer?

325. "The aristocrat of them all" was an advertising slogan for which beer and brewery?

326. Which beer was called the "Monarch of Them All" in its brewery's advertising?

327. What Toledo brewery described its beer as "Prince of Beers"?

328. What Minnesota brewer produced Royal 58 beer?

329. What Royal beer was sold by Geo. Wiedemann Brewing Company of Newport, Kentucky?

330. What brewery in New Athens, Illinois, produced Prince of Pilsen beer?

331. Cincinnati, Ohio, is known as the Queen City. What two breweries produced Queen City Beer?

Brewed just for you . . .

332. What beer was advertised as "The one beer to have when you're having more than one"?

333. This Winona, Minnesota, brewery claimed its beer "makes it fun to be thirsty."

334. What was "The friendly beer for modern people" from Reading, Pennsylvania?

335. What beer was advertised as "It's cool brewed" and "America's quality beer"?

336. The ads for this West Virginia beer said that it "brings you good cheer."

337. What Evansville, Indiana, beer's advertisements called it "The beer drinkers beer"?

338. What Duluth, Minnesota beer was called "the beer that Elmer drinks" in its advertisements?

339. What New York beer's ads said it would give you "that smile of pleasure"?

340. Who brewed Twenty Grand Ale and advertised it as "A man's brand"?

341. What was billed "The beer for the man who knows" from Minneapolis, Minnesota?

342. What brewery claimed to be "The thirst choice of the nation"?

343. What Boston brewer said its cream ale "Goes with the best of everything"?

344. What Pennsylvania brewer said of its beer, "It makes friends"?

345. What brewery produced Carnegie Pils'ner and Lager and advertised them as "The beers everyone likes"?

346. "The brew you'll enjoy—a century in every bottle" was a slogan of what brewery?

347. What was advertised as "The beer in the green bottle" from Detroit?

348. What brewery produced what they called the "Pilsener for me"?

349. Name what was advertised as "The beer for you" from Montana?

350. The beer that "serves you right."

351. They used the slogan "Try it—you always buy it."

352. This beer was advertised to quench your thirst because "it satisfies."

353. What brewery said, "We make a specialty of bottle beer for family trade"?

354. According to Spokane Brewing & Malting Company, this brand was "The kind your neighbor drinks."

355. Peter Doelger Brewing Company said its First Prize Bottle Beer was brewed expressly for what?

356. What Omaha, Nebraska, brewer produced Luxus beer prior to Prohibition and called it "The beer you like"?

357. "The drink for you" was how a Wisconsin brewer described what product?

358. "It tastes real" was a slogan for what Ohio beer made—according to advertising—from "four percent lager"?

359. What brewery used the slogan, "We made it good, you made it famous"?

360. What beer was advertised as "100% Union Made"?

Copy Cats

Copy cats

361. What was known as "Oklahoma's premium quality beer"?

362. This Kansas City, Missouri, brewing company said they offered "Quality since 1868."

363. This Wisconsin brewer claimed "Quality & flavor since 1849."

364. What brewer said its beer was "Famous for quality since 1873"?

365. What Port Jervis, New York, brewery advertised its beer as the "Beer of quality"?

366. What St. Paul, Minnesota, beer was "Famous for quality"?

367. What was the "Quality Beer & Ale" from New Jersey?

368. What Wisconsin brewer used the phrase "Quality since 1844" in its advertising?

369. This Milwaukee beer was described as "The beer of quality."

370. What New York brewery made "First Prize Quality Beer"?

371. Which Utah brewery described its pale beer as "Premium Quality"?

372. What were the brand and brewery associated with the "Beer of quality" from Erie, Pennsylvania?

373. Which beer "Made Milwaukee Famous"?

374. What beer was the beer that "Made Milwaukee Jealous"?

375. What was "The beer that made Omaha Jealous"?

376. What Washington brewery used the much parodied slogan "It's the water"?

377. Who countered Olympia's "It's the water" slogan with "It's the beer"?

378. What Washington brewery used the slogan "It's the material" for its Premo brand beer?

379. This brewery's brand Kloster Brau was advertised as "It's the beer."

To Your Health

To your health

380. Name the beer known as "The beer that builds" from Cleveland, Ohio.

381. What LaCrosse, Wisconsin, beer was said to be as "wholesome as sunshine"?

382. Name a Springfield, Illinois, beer advertised to be "For Health & Strength."

383. What brewery produced and touted Park Malt Tonic as the beer that "Makes you eat, helps you sleep"?

384. Which brewery produced Becco, which they called as "nourishing as beer"?

385. Banquet, called "The beer for you," and Vimalt, tagged "The health tonic," were products of what brewer?

386. This Illinois brewery said its lager was "The beer that builds you up."

387. Moerschel Spring Brewing Company said this about its pre-Prohibition brand White Pearl Beer.

388. What beer brand was advertised by the Houston Ice & Brewing Company as "The beer that builds you up"?

389. "The beer that builds" was what New Jersey beer's slogan?

390. Name this California beer said to be brewed "For health."

It Tastes Good

It tastes good

391. What is the world's strongest beer?

392. What state leads the United States in number of bars per capita?

393. What is the alcohol content of U.S. premium beers?

394. What strength beer can be purchased on U.S. military bases?

395. Which is more fattening: a twelve ounce bottle of beer or a twelve-ounce bottle of Coca-Cola?

396. In 1977 this brewery introduced the Beer Ball, a five and a half gallon container for beer.

397. Which brewery first applied the term "light beer" to low-calorie beer?

398. Which brewery introduced the first low-calorie beer?

399. What is a boilermaker?

400. Who brewed and what was the name of the eight ounce can of beer that was said to be "calorie-controlled" and the "original beer for women"?

401. What was touted as "The beer with the million dollar flavor" from Terre Haute, Indiana?

Like the Good Ol' Days

Like the good ol' days

402. What Cincinnati, Ohio, beer was said to have been "Aged in the hills"?

403. What Pennsylvania brewery produced Old Reliable Beer?

404. What beer claims to offer "Old fashioned goodness"?

405. This beer was said to have "age old flavor."

406. What was advertised as "The brew with that old time flavor"?

407. What beer, produced by the Indiana Brewing Company of Indianapolis, Indiana, was advertised as being "Like the good old days"?

408. Name a beer made by the San Diego Brewing Company that was advertised as "Traditionally good."

409. What beer was called "The brew that brings back memories"?

410. Old Anchor Beer was a product of what Pennsylvania brewer?

411. What Chicago brewery produced Old Chicago Beer?

412. Pennsylvania brewers Ashland, Brackenridge, Du Bois, Lockport, Union, Betz, Pittsburgh, and others all produced this "old" beer. What was it?

413. What beer did Grace Brothers of Santa Rosa, California, produce from 1956 to 1961 that had the same name as a cigarette?

414. Old Milwaukee was a long surviving brand name for Schlitz Brewing. What other Wisconsin brewer used this brand name?

415. What "old" beer from a Brooklyn, New York, brewer featured a windmill on the can?

We Have
the Edge

We have the edge

416. This Chicago brewer used the slogan "The Lightweight Champ" to promote its extra-light beer.

417. What Chicago brewery claimed to make "America's most imitated beer"?

418. They claimed their beer was "A miracle of fine brewing."

419. It was advertised as "The beer" from Chicago.

420. What beer was advertised as "One of America's 2 great beers"?

421. What Colorado brewer advertised "America's fine light beer"?

422. What Nebraska brewer advertised "America's light refreshing beer"?

423. This beer was advertised as "One of America's really fine beers."

424. This Detroit brewery advertised "The beer of distinction." Name the brand and brewery.

425. Name what was touted "That grand old beer" by a New York City brewer.

426. What brewery used the slogan "It stands on top"?

427. Name a St. Louis beer that claimed that it was "Seldom equaled, never excelled."

428. "Leads them all" was a slogan applied to what beer from a Milwaukee brewer?

429. A beer advertised as "The cream of table beers."

430. This pre-Prohibition brewery said of its beer, "none better."

431. This Kentucky beer was advertised as—"Wins by test."

432. Which brewery advertised Adler Brau Beer with "Request the best ... for friends and guests"?

Who's the best?

433. In New Orleans what brewer advertised the "Best beer in town"?

434. They claimed their beer was the "Best East or West."

435. "Beer at its best" was a slogan of what Brooklyn, New York, brewer?

436. Name the Wisconsin brewer that claimed to make the beer with "The finest flavor."

437. Name a Philadelphia beer which was dubbed "Best of all" by the brewer.

438. They claimed to have the "best beer in town" and the "best beer in the state."

439. This Nelsonville, Ohio, brewery claimed to make "The Best Beer."

440. Name the beer that was labeled "Best by every test."

441. What brewery produced Badger Brew and advertised it as "The best yet"?

442. In Sacramento, California, what was touted as the "Best beer brewed"?

443. What Iowa brewery advertised "Western Brew, Best in the West"?

444. They said their Barbarossa beer was "The finest bottled beer brewed."

445. They said their bottle beers were "the best on the coast."

446. This Omaha, Nebraska, brewery advertised "The delicious artesian brew" and "The best beer in America." Name the beers and the brewery.

447. What brewery used the slogan "The Best What Gives"?

448. What brewery proclaimed its beer "Absolutely the Best Ever Brewed"?

449. What beer was advertised as "The Finest Beer in Town"?

450. What Chicago beer was advertised as "The Beer Supreme"?

Remember This?

Remember this?

451. Which brewery used the slogan "Kraeusen Brewed ... as of old"?

452. What Milwaukee beer was associated with the 1960s advertising slogan, "I'm from Milwaukee, and I oughta know"?

453. What Rhode Island brewer used the slogan, "Hi Neighbor! From one of America's great breweries"?

454. What beer would you ask for after shouting "Hey, Mabel!"?

455. "Gimmie a Gam" was a slogan for what beer?

456. "What'll you have?" was a slogan for what company?

457. This beer was advertised as "a swell beer" and "a whale of a beer."

458. This Philadelphia brewer included "Brewers since 1860" in its advertising.

459. This beer and brewery were named after a president and the product was advertised as being "Worthy of a great name."

460. Called "The Happy Hoppy Drink" in Pabst Brewing Company's Prohibition days advertising.

461. This Pennsylvania beer was called "The talk of the town."

462. Cases of this beer were advertised as "A case of good judgment."

463. "Golden Glow, It's the after glow" was a slogan of what Wisconsin brewer?

464. What brewer said they produced "Good Honest Beer"?

465. What was called "The home favorite" beer brewed by the South Bethlehem Brewing Company of Bethlehem, Pennsylvania?

466. What Pennsylvania beer was touted "The beer worth asking for"?

467. Name what was called "The better beer" from Johnstown, Pennsylvania.

468. What beer was advertised as "the most expensive taste in beer"?

469. Whose beers were labeled the "Celebrated beers" of Philadelphia?

470. Dusseldorfer, called "The world's standard of perfection," was brewed by what brewery?

471. The slogan "Beer that is beer" came from what Wisconsin brewer?

472. What beer was called "The standard of excellence"?

473. "It hits the spot" was a slogan for what breweries and brands?

Support Your Local Brewer

Support your local brewer

474. Which brewery is located on the Youghiogheny River in Pennsylvania?

475. What was touted the "Pride of the Monongahela Valley"?

476. What was called "The brew that grew with the great Northwest"?

477. What was known as "The beer of the South"?

478. What was advertised as "the real beer from the Great Lakes country"?

479. This beer was said to be "custom brewed for all Wisconsin."

480. Name the beer that was labeled "from Chesapeake Bay, land of pleasant living."

481. What beer is said to be "made with Chippewa water from the Big Eddy Spring"?

482. This beer claimed to be "brewed with Waukesha water."

483. What was called "The only Eastern beer made in the West"?

484. What beer was advertised as the "Western way to say welcome"?

485. What brewery used the word *Zinzinnati* in its advertising campaign?

486. This Pennsylvania coal-country brewer claimed its beer was "Famous as anthracite."

487. What brewery used the slogan "Call for the brew from Kalamazoo"?

488. What brewery produced what was called "The Famous Utica Beer"?

489. What was known as "Buffalo's famous brew"?

490. Name the beer that was touted "Omaha's Favorite Beer."

491. Greylock Ale was advertised as "Made in the Berkshires." What brewery brewed it?

492. What beer was called the "Pride of the Black Hills"?

493.   What was touted the "Pride of Rochester"?

494.   What was known as "The beer of Akron"?

495.   What is the beer said to be "from the land of sky blue waters"?

496.   What beer was called the "Pride of Newark"?

497.   What beer was advertised as "The Pride of the Cincinnati Brewing Tradition"?

498.   What beer is labeled "Texas Own"?

499.   What beer is "Brewed with pure Rocky Mountain spring water"?

500.   What beer was advertised as "Cincinnati's Finest" and "Made in Cincinnati's most modern brewery"?

Answers

1. In 1587 by the Virginia colonists at the Roanoke colony of Sir Walter Raleigh. In his book *A Brief and True Report of the New Found Land of Virginia,* historian Thomas Harriot wrote, "Wee made of the same ... some mault, whereof was brued as good ale as was to bee desired."

2. Yes. An ancient Assyrian tablet concerning Noah translates in part: "For our food, I slaughtered oxen and killed sheep—day by day. With beer and brandy, oil and wine I filled large jars...."

3. French chemist and biologist Louis Pasteur (1822–1895).

4. The third President of the United States, Thomas Jefferson (1743–1826), who brewed beer at his Monticello estate in Virginia from 1813–1826.

5. Munroe Tavern.

6. The twenty-first. In light of the event, on April 7, 1933, *The New York Times* was headlined "BEER FLOWS IN 19 STATES AT MIDNIGHT."

Actually, beer was then legalized in twenty states and the District of Columbia.

7. There are several stories regarding King Gambrinus and details vary. Some say he was a mythical Flemish King; others Dutch; and others English. Some say the name may have been derived from the twelfth century Belgian nobleman and brewer, Jan Primus. Some call him St. Gambrinus, the patron saint of beer. What *is* true, is that a likeness of a man wearing a crown and dubbed King Gambrinus appears on the labels of several breweries and adorned several breweries in the past in the form of a statue. Breweries named Gambrinus were located in Chicago, Illinois (1900–1936); St. Louis, Missouri (1857–1863); Buffalo, New York (1891–1904); New York, New York (1883–1943); Cincinnati, Ohio (1876–1919); Columbus, Ohio (1906–1919); Toledo, Ohio (1902–1904); Portland, Oregon (1889–1916); New Kensington, Pennsylvania (1897–1904); and Oshkosh, Wisconsin (1875–1894).

8. The beer can was introduced by American Can Company and Krueger Brewing Company.

9. Keeler Tavern.

10. Falcon Tavern in Bankside.

11. January 16, 1920, at midnight.

12. Buckman Tavern.

13. They dumped 100,000 gallons of Rheingold Beer into New York City's East River. Increased taxes had made it more difficult to compete with out-of-state brewers, which were increasing their shipments to the New York market. The problem continued and, in 1974, the Rheingold Brewery was closed.

14. The eighteenth, which was ratified on January 29, 1919.

15. National Prohibition, 1920–1933. It was an experiment that cost the country, according to government statistics, $34,565,109,245.00 as a result of lost tax revenue and enforcement costs.

16. 1826 in Boston, Massachusetts.

17. Tabard Inn.

18. The soft-top aluminum end was introduced.

19. 1933. Beer became legal in twenty states by April. National repeal was in effect by December, when the amendment was ratified to the Constitution. The term *repeal* became a household word and the era following Prohibition has often been dubbed *repeal.*

20. 1810. Oktoberfest is an annual tradition in Germany (in October!) and swells the population of Munich for the celebration.

21. 1919.

22. The Cullen Bill, a major step toward the repeal of Prohibition. The strength of beer is expressed in alcoholic content by volume. 3.2 beer is a low-alcohol beer compared to the average beer at 4.5 percent alcohol by volume.

23. Oregon in 1972.

24. Near beers produced during Prohibition (Pabst, Schlitz, Miller, Strohs, and Anheuser-Busch). Other Pabst near beers were Hoppy, Yip, and Ona. A near beer is a cereal beverage with alcoholic content removed to less than 0.5 percent.

25. Carrie Nation, member of the Women's Christian Temperance Union. Between 1900 and 1911, Carrie was arrested thirty times for what she called "Hatchetations" but what police called "disturbing the peace." In 1867 twenty-one-year-old Carrie married an alcoholic who instilled in her the aversion to drink. She eventually became known as the "Loving home defender" as a result of her well-publicized demonstration against drinking.

26. The wood pulp coaster.

27. Vassar College, the first privately endowed college for women. Matthew's 408 thousand dollar founding contribution is celebrated in a Vassar song: "And so you see the old V.C./ Our love shall never fail/Full well we know/ That all we owe to Matthew Vassar's ale!"

28. Chicago in 1869. In 1872 the Prohibition Party offered its first presidential candidate, James Polack. He pulled less than six thousand votes. In 1892 candidate John Bidwell received 271,058 votes. Numbers never increased significantly, and since Prohibition, the highest was a bit over one hundred thousand votes in 1948. The Prohibition Party is the longest-lived third party in the history of the United States.

29. The Chicago fire of 1871, which started in the barn of Patrick O'Leary and has often been blamed on Mrs. O'Leary's cow. The cow supposedly kicked over a lantern.

30. American Society for the Promotion of Temperance (also known as the American Temperance Society).

31. Green beer. During the aging process, protein and yeast settle out and carbon dioxide is generated. The flavor will improve as the beer ages. Proper aging takes several weeks to several months depending on the type of beer.

32. It is a fermenting agent that turns the wort to beer. (Wort is the liquid that results from the boiling of grain.)

33. 31.

34. Yeast. This frothy substance consists of a mass of minute fungi, which germinate and multiply in the presence of starch or sugar and form alcohol.

35. Pilsener. Pilsen is where it was originally brewed. American beers resemble the Pilsener type as they are light and hoppy.

36. Barley, malt, hops, yeast, and water.

37. Zymurgy, from the Greek words *zymo*, "leaven", and *ergon*, "work."

38. Rice—simply because it is lighter in color than the other grains, and thus does not add color to the brew.

39. Ale is a top-fermented beer brewed from malt cereal. Top-fermented beers are brewed at warm temperatures (58°–70°F) and, as a result, the fermenting agent, yeast, remains on top. Lager beers are stored in cool areas during fermentation. At cold temperatures (below 58°F), yeast sinks and thus the term bottom-fermented beer is applied to lagers.

40. 3,968. There are 31 gallons of beer in a barrel, 4 quarts to a gallon, and 32 ounces per quart. $31 \times 4 \times 32 = 3,968$!

41. Carbon dioxide. When a tap on a keg is opened, the carbon dioxide in the beer expands and the beer is forced out. Carbon dioxide is a product of the fermentation process (that's what makes the bubbles!).

42. Wort.

43. A vine herb. Hops are not only important to beer's flavor and aroma, but also are an important factor in preventing spoilage of beer by curbing the growth of bacteria.

44. Malt.

45. Hops.

46. Stout beer. It is made with the top-fermentation method of brewing.

47. Olde Frothingslosh. The Pittsburgh Brewing Company produced Olde Frothingslosh as a gag beer (the foam is not really on the bottom). It was introduced in 1954. The labels still feature the 300-pound go-go dancer Fatima Yechburg.

48. Grain Belt from Minneapolis, Minnesota. Grain Belt was purchased by G. Heileman Brewing Company of LaCrosse, Wisconsin, in 1976.

49. Theodore Hamm Brewing Company, St. Paul, Minnesota.

50. Franklin Brewing Company, Columbus, Ohio. Obviously, the beer was not 100 percent grain;

it also needed water. Advertising agencies have taken many liberties over the years when writing beer advertising claims!

51. Koerber Beer from Koerber Brewing Company, Toledo, Ohio, 1933–1949.

52. Lucky Lager by the West Coast's General Brewing Corporation.

53. Miami Valley Brewing Company, Dayton, Ohio, 1933–1950.

54. Steinle Beer from Steinle Brewing & Ice Company. This brewery, founded in 1858, lasted into Prohibition until 1927. An attempt to restart the brewery in 1934 failed.

55. Goetz Company. The owner, William Goetz, was one of the cofounders of the American Brewers Association in 1930.

56. Zoller's Beer from Zoller Brewing Company. The Zoller brand name was used from 1935–1944. This brewery later became the Blackhawk Brewing Company (1944) and then Uchtorff Brewing Company (1952). It closed in 1955.

57. Walter Brewing Company of Pueblo from 1933–1971. They also proclaimed their beer was "brewed with pure Rocky Mountain spring water"—the same slogan used by Coors of Golden, Colorado, today.

58. Wagner's beer from Sidney, Ohio. This family operation was founded by Joseph Wagner in 1854. It closed for Prohibition and reopened in 1936. It survived only until 1939.

59. Old Style Lager from Heileman Brewing Company, LaCrosse, Wisconsin.

60. Chief Oshkosh from Oshkosh Brewing Company, Oshkosh, Wisconsin.

61. Burgermeister from Burgermeister Brewing Corporation in Los Angeles and San Francisco. *Burgermeister* is the German word for mayor.

62. Fortune Bros. of Chicago, Illinois, 1857–1948. Fortune Brothers survived Prohibition by manufacturing spaghetti and macaroni.

63. Menominee-Marinette Brewing Company, Menominee, Michigan. This brewery was closed in 1961.

64. Duquesne Brewing Company, Pittsburgh, Pennsylvania. The Duquesne name was purchased by Schmidt's of Philadelphia in 1972.

65. Christian Heurich Brewing Company, Washington, D.C. The brewery was demolished in 1962 and land for the Center was donated in 1965.

66. Yuengling of Pottsville, Pennsylvania, has been operated by the Yuengling family since its foundation in 1829 by David G. Yuengling.

67. Stroh Brewery Company under the name Stroh Products Co. In 1984 Stroh was the third largest brewer in the United States with a production of 23.9 million barrels of beer.

68. Labatt Brewing Company. The tractors were used for beer deliveries.

69. Miller Brewing Company.

70. The Old Fort Brewery in Prince George, British Columbia, Canada.

71. Schlitz in 1954.

72. Rheingold, Brooklyn, New York. Using girls in Rheingold advertising was nothing new—prior to Prohibition, they used the Rheingold Girl.

73. John Gund Brewing Company, LaCrosse, Wisconsin. In 1858 John Gund started a brewery with Gottlieb Heileman and sold his interest in 1872 to start his own brewery. The Gund brewery survived until 1920. The Heileman brewery is still in operation.

74. St. Marys Beverage Company, St. Marys, Pennsylvania. The brewery closed for Prohibition from 1920 to 1933 and lasted seven years after Prohibition.

75. Montana Brewing Company, Great Falls, Montana, 1893–1918.

76. Globe.

77. Miller Brewing Company. Philip Morris took over the brewery in 1970, but Miller's headquarters remain in Milwaukee. In 1984, Miller was the country's second largest brewer with a production of 37.9 million barrels of beer.

78. Pabst (Jacob Best) and Miller (Charles and Lorenz Best—sons of Jacob). Jacob Best started his brewery at 917 Chestnut Street in 1844. The Miller Brewing Company had its roots in the Plank Road Brewery in Wauwatosa in 1850.

79. Bartels Breweries of Syracuse, New York (closed 1942), and Edwardsville, Pennsylvania (closed 1968).

80. Pickett of Dubuque, Iowa; and Potosi of Potosi, Wisconsin.

81. Sunset Brewing Company of Wallace, Idaho, from 1901–1917. After Prohibition the brewery operated under the names Sunset and DeLuxe from 1934–1949.

82. James Bohannan of Peerless Motor Car Company gave up auto production in 1932 and converted the plant to a brewery after Prohibition. It was known as the Brewing Corporation of America until 1953, when it was purchased by Carling Brewing Company. In 1971 Philadelphia brewer Christian Schmidt purchased it and operated it until 1984.

83. Schultz and Dooley, who were popularized in the period 1959–1966 by the West End Brewing Company of Utica, New York.

84. Coors of Golden, Colorado.

85. Pickett Brewing Company of Dubuque, Iowa.

86. DuBois Brewing Company, DuBois, Pennsylvania. The advertising for their "Budweiser" beer stated "Every drop of this premium beer is brewed with pure mountain spring water."

87. Gretz Brewing Company of Philadelphia in the fifties.

88. F. W. Cook Company of Evansville, Indiana.

89. Schlitz in February 1963.

90. Pabst in July 1935. They canned their export label first and later their leading Blue Ribbon brand was canned.

91. Dr. Miller Company, Crete Brewery 1934–1942.

92. Yoerg Brewing Company. Yoerg was the pioneer of lager brewing in St. Paul. In early brewing days before sophisticated refrigeration techniques, aging beer in caves or cellars was necessary to keep the beer from going sour.

93. Belmont Brewing Company, Martins Ferry, Ohio. The brewery was founded in 1890 as the Belmont Brewing Company and survived until 1940. During Prohibition it was known as Belmont Products Company.

94. Jacob Ruppert, who was always ready to satisfy. A strong spokesman against the enforcers of Prohibition, Ruppert said in 1922, "The leading New York brewers expect the return of beer and are ready to turn out the real stuff."

95. Atlas Brewing Co.

96. Horlacher of Allentown, Pennsylvania. This beer was an area favorite for many years. The brewery closed in 1978, after 66 years in business.

97. Apache (1933–1949).

98. Labatt's. It was test-marketed for a short time in the late sixties.

99. Light & Mellow.

100. Brew 92 produced by General Brewing Company.

101. Iron City of Pittsburgh, Pennsylvania.

102. Tango.

103. Chelsea. This short-lived product was unable to compete with the giants in the soft drink industry.

104. Pace by Hudepohl introduced in 1983 and Break by Schmidt introduced in 1984.

105. Nude Beer from New Jersey's Eastern Brewing Corp. The idea was conceived by William Boam of Tustin, California. When he proposed a beer label picturing a bare-breasted woman, the Alcohol Control Department ruled against it. He did, however, get the okay to have a label with a girl clad in a scratch-off bikini.

106. Bevo, which was produced until 1929. At Prohibition, Busch also announced that part of its plant would be involved in the manufacture of high-grade packinghouse products.

107. Stroh's.

108. Tannhaeuser. It was introduced by Obert in 1876 and used from 1936–1941 by Uhl. The opera was based on the legend of a thirteenth century German knight who sought absolution after a bit of revelry.

109. Lucky Lager. Incidentally, it is a West Coast brew, and the setting of the movie was the Southeast!

110. They all produced Billy Beer, named after President James Carter's brother Billy. The labels quote Billy: "I had this beer brewed up just for you. I think it's the best I ever tasted. And I've tasted a lot. I think you'll like it, too."

111. They were all sold with paper labels at one time.

112. Playmate Beer, 1967–1968.

113. James Bond's 007 Beer, made by the National Brewing Company's Phoenix, Arizona, branch from 1967–1969.

114. Mr. Lager.

115. Black Pride from 1967–1972. It was advertised as "A beer as proud as its people."

116. Soul Malt Liquor and Soul Mellow Yellow. Both were distributed in late 1967, two years after the riots.

117. Orbit of Miami, Florida, and Astro of Los Angeles, California.

118. Walter's Beer from Walter Brewing Company of Pueblo, Colorado.

119. Pabst. In 1882 Pabst started tying blue ribbons around the neck of bottles of beer that were of superior quality and called Select. But it was not until the 1890s that the beer was officially named Pabst Blue Ribbon.

120. Krueger from Krueger Brewing Company, Newark, New Jersey, in 1935.

121. Miller.

122. Gold Top from Hoster-Columbus, Columbus, Ohio.

123. Falstaff. The name derives from Sir John Falstaff, the fat, jovial, witty knight in William Shakespeare's *Henry IV* and *The Merry Wives of Windsor*.

124. Wee Willy. The brewery operated from 1881–1966.

125. The Miller Brewing Company has used the trademark since 1903.

126. Hensler from Newark, New Jersey. Hensler went out of business in 1958. A whale also appears on cans of Whales White Ale from National Brewing Company of Baltimore (1970–1973).

127. The Professor.

128. 1872. It was registered with the United States Patent Office on May 8, 1877.

129. Victor Brewing Company. Victor was purchased in 1941 by the Fort Pitt Brewing Company of Sharpsburg and closed in 1955.

130. A tuba player. The beer was brewed from 1934–1973.

131. Gretz Brewing Company. The Gretz slogan was "Made the Old-Fashioned Way—Slowly—Naturally."

132. The Nightwalker.

133. "Purity, Body, and Flavor." The trademark was adopted by Ballantine of Newark, New Jersey, in 1879.

134. According to Eberhard Anheuser, the founder's grandson, "The *A* stands for Anheuser and the Eagle symbolizes Adolphus Busch whose vision knew no horizon."

135. G. Krueger Brewing Company of Newark, New Jersey.

136. Iroquois (later the International Brewing Company). Iroquois purchased the brewery in 1892 from the Roos Cooperative Brewery. The brewery, founded in 1830 by Jacob Roos, was Buffalo's first.

137. Old Topper Ale and Beer from Rochester Brewing Company of Rochester, New York. A man in a top hat also appears on cans of Town Club Lager Beer from Interstate Brewing Company, Vancouver, Washington (1939–1950).

138. A waiter.

139. Piel Brothers of Brooklyn, New York.

140. Wooden Shoe Brewing Company (1939–1954) of Minster, Ohio. This small brewery was founded by Frank Lange in 1869, operated as the Star Brewing Company from 1890–1919, and after Prohibition until 1939 operated as Star Beverage Company.

141. Schlitz.

142. Joseph W. Ortlieb of Henry Ortlieb Brewing Company. Joseph was chief executive and owner of the company during the seventies and until it was sold to Christian Schmidt Brewing Company in 1981.

143. Pearl XXX Beer.

144. Bert and Harry Piels for Piel Brothers of Brooklyn, New York; and Godfrey Gunther, Sr., and Junior for Gunther Brewing in Maryland.

145. Schaefer.

146. Fred MacMurray. He is perhaps best remembered by television viewers for his role as the father in the series *My Three Sons,* and he also appeared in a number of Hollywood movies.

147. Mel Allen. Ballantine was a major sponsor of sporting events.

148. Chuck Berry.

149. Comedian Jonathan Winters.

150. Each of these men married the boss's daughter and became important names in brewing history. In 1861 Adolphus Busch married Anheuser's daughter and he was taken into the business. Philip Best passed his business on to son-in-law Fred Pabst in 1864. And in 1876 Adam Gettelman took over the business founded by his father-in-law George Schweikhart.

151. Adolphus Busch was the principal owner of the Lone Star Brewery in 1891. In 1893 he became president of the brewery. The Busch name was also known in Dallas for the ownership of the Adolphus Hotel.

152. The Greek philosopher Aristotle (B.C. 384–322).

153. Labatt Brewing Company.

154. Max von Sydow, a Swedish actor, perhaps better known for his roles in *The Greatest Story Ever Told, Hawaii,* and *The Exorcist.*

155. Jinx Falkenburg, who was selected in 1940.

156. F. X. Matt II of Matt Brewing Company (formerly West End Brewing Company) of Utica, New York.

157. Andy Capp by Reg Smythe.

158. William Shakespeare.

159. Christian Heurich of Chr. Heurich Brewing Company of Washington, D.C.

160. Billy Carter of Billy Beer fame. Billy Beer was "Brewed expressly for and with the personal approval of one of America's all-time great beer drinkers—Billy Carter."

161. Joseph Schlitz, who was a bookkeeper in the employ of Krug. Schlitz drowned at sea in 1875 and control of the brewery fell to the Uihlein family, the nephews of August Krug. The Uihlein family maintained control but kept the Schlitz name. In 1981, the Milwaukee Brewery was closed. In 1982 all remaining interests were sold to the Stroh Brewing Company of Detroit.

162. Budweiser cans. He estimates he will need 10,000 by completion.

163. *Deliverance.*

164. Art Carney. He is probably best known for his role as Ed Norton in *The Honeymooners* television series with Jackie Gleason.

165. They all encouraged the manufacture and consumption of beer by actively promoting appropriate legislation.

166. F. X. Matt II of Matt Brewing Company of Utica, New York.

167. *Strange Brew.*

168. Al Capone of Chicago.

169. Thomas Jefferson from 1813–1826.

170. Gulf Brewing Company, the brewers of Grand Prize Beer. The brewery was founded in 1933, purchased by Theodore Hamm Brewing Company of St. Paul in 1963, and closed in 1967.

171. Globe Brewing Company of Baltimore. The beer was produced under the name Hals Brewing Company. When the Globe brewery was erected in 1744 by Captain Leonard, it was the largest brewery in America.

172. First President of the United States, George Washington (1732–1799).

173. Diane Baker, who appeared in *The Diary of Anne Frank, Marnie, Straitjacket* and other films.

174. The lift tab, ring pull, and other easy opening devices for cans.

175. General Israel Putnam. He is best known for his often quoted line, "Don't fire until you see the whites of their eyes!"

176. Preserving food in vessels of tin. This was the start of the canning industry.

177. A hurricane. The carpenter was John Gretchen III in a *Life* magazine interview.

178. Ronald Reagan (with his permission!).

179. Barrels.

180. Woman's Christian Temperance Union. Founded in 1874, the organization sought to end liquor traffic and helped lead to the Pro-

hibition amendment. In the 1970s, eight thousand chapters of the WCTU were active in the United States.

181. William Painter of Baltimore, Maryland. In 1892 while in the employ of the Crown Cork and Seal Company, he invented a tin cover containing a thin cork that sealed the bottle.

182. Andrew Volstead from Minnesota. The Volstead Act of 1919 defined "intoxicating liquor" as any beverage containing more than one-half of one percent alcohol.

183. John Wagner. This happened in 1840 in Philadelphia at 455 Saint John Street.

184. John Madden.

185. James Coburn. He is well-known for his character Flint in the James Bond spoofs.

186. At the 1893 Chicago World's Fair. This fair was officially named the World's Columbian Exposition celebrating the four hundredth anniversary of the discovery of America.

187. Lone Star Cotton Mills. The brewhouse was located in San Antonio, Texas.

188. Mathaser Hall is the Lowenbrau brewery hall. It is the largest in the world and can seat seven thousand people for Oktoberfest celebrations.

189. Fraunces Tavern, New York, New York. Washington's farewell address took place on December 4, 1783. The tavern is located at the southeast corner of Broad and Pearl Streets.

190. A 5½ foot beer bottle.

191. Italy.

192. The Brown Bottle. Another Schlitz landmark in Milwaukee was the Schlitz Hotel and Palm Garden, built in 1889.

193. Pickett Brewing Company of Dubuque, Iowa.

194. Stevens Point, Wisconsin, where Point Special Beer is brewed.

195. The Berghoff.

196. Zigi's.

197. Raleigh Tavern in Williamsburg.

198. Louisiana State University. The name honored the team for their 10–0 record in 1958. Beer was brewed by the Jackson Brewing Company of New Orleans.

199. Maine, New Jersey, New Mexico, North Carolina, North Dakota, South Carolina, and South Dakota. Mississippi never had a brewery but there were "Mississippi" breweries in Iowa, Minnesota, and Missouri.

200. Chicago. Capone was an Italian-born gangster who gained control of gambling, vice, and bootlegging during Chicago's Prohibition days. In his own defense he said, "All I ever did was to sell whiskey to our best people."

201. Coshocton, Ohio (by J. F. Meek in the late nineteenth century).

202. Denver, Colorado. Mile Hi was the name of the brewery operated by the Consumers Brewing Company at Wazee and 36th Street from 1909–1910. From 1910–1915 it was Capitol Brewing Company. The Mile Hi Label was used by the Tivoli Brewing Company of Denver in the 1960s.

203. Detroit from 1911–1919 and from 1933–1942. It was closed during Prohibition.

204. Mississippi.

205. The Japanese word for beer. Popular Japanese beers currently imported to the United States are Asahi, Kirin, Sapporo, and Suntory.

206. An ale taster. This is one of England's oldest public offices. It was created by William the Conqueror.

207. India pale ale. The beer was produced in England and shipped to the colonists. Several U.S. and Canadian breweries applied the term to their beer. Labatt's of Canada still brews an India pale ale.

208. Weiss beer. (Weiss is the German word for white.)

209. The Spanish word for beer. *Cerveza* has its origins in the Latin words *Ceres*, "goddess of grain" and *vis*, "vigor." Spain produces no memorable beers; however, the U.S. beer drinker may have had an occasion to order Mexican beers, such as Carta Blanca, Dos Equis, Corona, or Tecate.

210. A tied house.

211. They are tools used by coopers to make barrels. The downright is used to shave the outside of the stave and the block hook is used to hold the staves in a barrel while they are being shaped.

212. Bridal. On her wedding day, the bride would distribute rounds of ale for which friends and guests were expected to contribute money to assist her in setting up housekeeping. The custom was known as Bride-Ale.

213. A tin bucket that was used to take draught beer home from the neighborhood tavern. An article in the July 20, 1888, issue of the *New York Herald* discusses the employment in factories of boys and girls ages ten-thirteen who were hired to fetch beer in *growlers*. A 1940s quart cone-top can from Chicago's Manhattan Brewing Company pictured a dog under the word *Growler* and a 1940s twenty-four ounce can of Old Milwaukee Beer was marked *Growler*.

214. Light beers and dark beers.

215. *Bière.* The most popular French beer exported to the United States is Kronenbourg, which was founded in 1664—thus the label "Kronenbourg 1664 Imported Beer."

216. Alewife.

217. A *tuplak.*

218. Beers produced in Japan for the domestic and export market.

219. Rosebud.

220. Ninety-nine (initially!).

221. *America.* Do you know what the initials *F & M* in F & M Schaefer Brewing Company stands for? Frederick Schaefer came to the United States in 1838 and bought the brewery of Sebastian Sommers in 1842 with his brother Maxmilian, and thus the F & M.

222. Genuine.

223. A device for opening cans that was introduced in 1965. (A great source of litter throughout the United States!)

224. Wet. A 1912 Prohibitionist song goes, "Nobody knows the way I vote,/The 'Wets' think I vote wet,/Nobody knows the way I vote,/The 'Drys' think I vote dry;/Fiddle-de-dee, fiddle-de-dee, /you can't fool me;/The man who won't tell how he votes,/he always votes for whisky."

225. *Bier.* The U.S. beer drinker will quickly recognize German beer names such as Beck's, Dortmunder, Henninger, Lowenbrau, St. Pauli, and Wurzburger.

226. Draft beer.

227. Stein.

228. Pilsner. The name is derived from the town of Pilsen, Czechoslovakia, where Pilsner beer was first produced. Pilsner is paler and more bitter than a lager beer.

229. A brewery.

230. An ancient drink of fermented honey and water. Sanskrit records from as early as 3000 B.C. mention mead.

231. A brewery in France. (*Brasserie* is the French word for brewery.)

232. A large beer barrel varying in capacity from 100–140 gallons.

233. Internal Revenue Tax Paid.

234. An unpasteurized beer normally packaged in kegs and barrels.

235. Dry. A 1912 Prohibitionist Dry song goes, "We ring the challenge out, All evil hosts defying;/ Our battle cry we shout, with colors proudly flying./Prohibition forever! Prohibition for-forever!/The battle cry we shout is Prohibition forever!"

236. Breweriana.

237. To scrape foam off the top of a pitcher or mug of beer (also known as a foam scraper or foam skimmer).

238. The Latin word *bibere* meaning "to drink."

239. Storehouse. (Lager beer must age in a cool place.)

240. "Watch your P's and Q's." This was a notice to barmaids and customers to keep track of their tab.

241. A rooster.

242. A bulldog.

243. A dog (pointer!).

244. A squirrel.

245. Foolish Pleasure and Honest Pleasure.

246. The goat. (Bock is the German word for male goat.) Bock beer is a heavy, dark beer, which is brewed in the winter and sold in the spring.

247. A fox.

248. The Hamm's bear.

249. Lone Star Beer of San Antonio, Texas, is best known for it; however, in the early 1980s the small Spoetzel Brewery of Shiner, Texas, sold Czhilispiel beer and the label depicted an armadillo.

250. A rooster. Brewster was a trademark of the Goebel Brewing Company of Detroit, Michigan.

251. A bull.

252. A deer. (New Ulm is also the home of Hermann the German, which is a 102 foot statue overlooking the town. It honors Hermann the Chiruscan, who united the German tribes to defeat the Romans in 9 A.D.)

253. Narragansett Brewing Company.

254. The buffalo. Southern used the slogan, "Don't say beer, say buffalo."

255. Pheasant. Sebewaing's slogan was "Brewed with deep rock well water."

256. A tiger. Tiger Beer is also a brand name of C. Schmidt & Sons of Philadelphia. An empty Tiger Beer can from Manhattan Brewing Company sold in the 1980s for $6,000—a record price!

257. A mustang.

258. Waukesha, Wisconsin. It was brewed by Fox Head Brewing Company under the name One-Two Brewing Company from 1958–1961.

259. National Brewing Company of Baltimore, Detroit, and Phoenix; (Colt 45) and Dixie Brewing Company of New Orleans (Dixie 45).

260. Hudepohl Brewing Company.

261. 520. Louis Ziegler bought the Beaver Dam brewery from Julia Goeggerle in 1904, closed in 1920 at Prohibition, and reopened after Prohibition from 1933–1953.

262. Stegmaier Brewing Company of Wilkes-Barre, Pennsylvania. Stegmaier sold Stallion XII from 1966 to 1973.

263. Duluth Brewing & Malting Company of Duluth, Minnesota, which was founded in 1896. In 1920 it became known as Rex Sobriety Company and it remained that way through Prohibition until closing in 1966.

264. Bechauds Brewery of Fond du Lac, Wisconsin. This brewery was founded in 1871 by A. G. Bechaud and survived until 1941.

265. Oertel Brewing Company. The beer was Oertels 92 Beer. *92* stood for John Oertel's independence of 1892 when he bought out his partner Charles Hartmetz. Oertel operated until 1967.

266. Wayne Brewing Company of Erie, Pennsylvania. The brand was first produced in 1939 (therefore the name) and continued being brewed until 1944. The brewery closed in 1951.

267. Brownsville Brewing Company of Brownsville, Pennsylvania. The brewery operated from 1905–1920 and 1933–1935.

268. Milan Brewing Company of Milan, Ohio. Milan produced Old 93 Beer from 1943–1950.

269. Goldcrest 51 Beer.

270. 400.

271. Matz Brewing Company of Bellaire, Ohio. From 1905–1919, prior to Prohibition, this brewery was the Bellaire Brewing Company. After Prohibition, from 1937–1953, it operated as Matz Brewing Company.

272. Belmont Brewing Company of Martins Ferry, Ohio. Belmont was founded in 1890 and operated through Prohibition, from 1919–1933, as Belmont Products Company. It went out of business in 1940.

273. Star Brewing Company of Boston, Massachusetts. 1896 refers to the foundation year of the firm in the Roxbury section of Boston. The brewery operated until 1952.

274. Philadelphia Brewing Company of Philadelphia. The beer was produced from 1942–1949.

275. Wm. Peter Brewing Company of Union City, New Jersey. The beer was produced from 1933–1936. The brewery was established at Hudson Avenue and Weehawken Street by William Peter in 1859.

276. Genesee Brewing Company of Rochester, New York.

277. Gettelman and Miller of Milwaukee, Wisconsin. Gettelman was purchased by Miller in 1961.

278. 18-K Beer. Hudepohl of Cincinnati, Ohio, brewed a beer labeled 14-K.

279. F. W. Cook of Evansville, Indiana.

280. Goebel Brewing Company of Detroit, Michigan. An advertising slogan for Private Stock 22 was "Always a pleasure to serve."

281. Maier Brewing Company of Los Angeles, California.

282. The first can being manufactured in Massachusetts.

283. Acme, Grace, Maier, and California in California; Drewrys in Indiana; Atlas in Chicago.

284. Alcoa. Iron City Beer was marketed in the cans.

285. Frontenac Beer. National Breweries, Ltd., of Montreal, Quebec, marketed this beer in cone-topped cans. Flat-top cans did not make an appearance in Canada until 1949, when Molson released its Export Label.

286. Frank Fehr Brewing Company.

287. King of diamonds. Other cards in beer advertising include a thirteen-card hand on cans of Trump Ale from Wehle Brewing Company of West Haven, Connecticut; a heart royal flush on Royal Beer cans from Reno Brewing Company; a tray from South Bethlehem Brewing Company of Pennsylvania showing dogs tearing up cards; and a Leisy Beer (Peoria, Illinois) tray showing a ten-card gin hand.

288. F. W. Cook's Goldblume Beer from 1933 to 1972.

289. Boston Beer Company on Boston Light cans from 1933–1957.

290. Beverwyck Brewing Company. Beverwyck was founded in 1867. In 1950 the brewery was purchased by the F & M Schaefer Brewing Company of Brooklyn, New York. Schaefer closed the brewery in 1972.

291. Van Merritt from 1953–1955.

163

292. Wiedemann produced a can that resembled the Budweiser can in color and in style. Anheuser-Busch used the word *Genuine* up the side and Wiedemann used the word *Original*.

293. 1957. Six cans were issued in 1957 picturing six contestants for Miss Rheingold. The winner in 1957 was Margie McNally. Miss Rheingold cans were not issued in subsequent years.

294. Gretz Brewing Company of Philadelphia, Pennsylvania.

295. Esslinger's of Philadelphia, Pennsylvania. In its advertising Esslinger also popularized the Little Man who was a waiter carrying a tray of beer.

296. The Boston Bruins. This was in honor of their Stanley Cup victory in 1970.

297. Altes Sportsman Ale.

298. Drewry's of South Bend, Indiana.

299. King Snedley Beer from Lucky Brewing Company of San Francisco from 1970–1972.

300. Iron City. It was test-marketed in Virginia first.

301. The sixteen ounce beer can.

302. Continental Can Company. They began the process in 1965.

303. American Can Company. It was a process for bonding can seams introduced in 1965.

304. A-1.

305. Pacific Can Company of California.

306. Capsealed, introduced in September 1935.

307. Crowntainer. This was a shorter and wider version of the cone top can. It was introduced in the early forties.

308. Keglined. This referred to a thin coating inside the can that kept the beer from reacting with the metal. These cans were introduced in 1935.

309. Beer cans supplied to the armed forces during World War II that had a black outline on olive drab background.

310. Continental Can Company for Schlitz in September 1935. In the years that followed, Continental Can manufactured these spout top cans in twelve-, sixteen-, and thirty-two-ounce sizes.

311. They both picture bull's-eyes or targets. Old Ranger (Hornell Brewing Company of Hornell, New York) added the line "It's a hit" on the cans. Bull's Eye was made by the Golden West Brewing Company of Oakland, California.

312. Krueger Cream Ale from Gottfried Krueger Brewing Company of Newark, New Jersey.

313. In 1935 through the combined efforts of the Krueger Brewing Company and American Can Company.

314. They were all celebrating their fiftieth year in 1985.

315. A horseshoe. A famous western Pennsylvania beer was Horse Shoe Curve Beer from Altoona Brewing Company. The labels picture the well-known Horse Shoe Curve railroad track.

316. An airplane. Grace Brothers of Santa Rosa, California produced Clipper Pale Beer from 1942–1950.

317. Mountains.

318. Schlitz in September 1935. A narrow spout much like a beer bottle made this can easily adaptable to brewery bottling lines for filling.

319. Pittsburgh Brewing Company in 1962. Iron City Beer was test-marketed in these Alcoa cans in Virginia first. Schlitz took the idea nationally a few months later.

320. Union Brewing Company at 506 Sampson Street in New Castle, Pennsylvania. The brewery closed its doors in 1948.

321. Kings Brewery of Brooklyn, New York. Kings was founded by Federick Hower on Pulaski Street in 1890. It operated during Prohibition as Excelsior Brewing Company and closed under the Kings name in 1938.

322. Regal from Regal Brewing Company.

323. Budweiser. Brewed by Anheuser-Busch, America's largest brewer, Budweiser's sales in 1984 topped 64 million barrels.

324. Montgomery Brewing Company of Montgomery from 1933–1937. The brewery closed in 1942.

325. Kingsbury Pale from Kingsbury Breweries Company of Manitowoc, Wisconsin.

326. Gold Nugget from Black Hills Brewing Company of Central City, South Dakota.

327. Home Brewing Company. Home was a pre-Prohibition company.

328. Duluth Brewing & Malting Company. The beer was produced from 1951–1965, and its advertising slogan was "Treat yourself royally."

329. Royal Amber. It was sold from 1945–1960.

330. Mound City Brewing Company. Prince of Pilsen was produced from 1933–1950.

331. Red Top of Cincinnati and Queen City Brewing of Cumberland, Maryland. Red Top Queen City was produced from 1933–1936 and Cumberland Queen City from 1941–1947.

332. Schaefer.

333. Peter Bub Brewing Company. The brewery was located in "the shadow" of Winona's Sugar Loaf Mountain.

334. Reading Beer from Reading Brewing Company. Another Reading slogan was "Brewed with clear Blue Mountain water." Reading is also known for a beer test can that simply had a question mark and the words "what brand" where a beer name would normally appear. At the bottom of the label it said "The refreshing taste will suggest the answer."

335. Heileman's Old Style of La Crosse, Wisconsin. In the 1970s and 1980s Heileman became one of the top United States brewers through a number of acquisitions of dying breweries.

336. Fesenmeier made by Fesenmeier Brewing Company of Huntington, West Virginia.

337. Sterling from Sterling Brewing Company.

338. Fitger's Legion Beer.

339. Ruppert. (The Ruppert name is well-known for Knickerbocker Beer. Knickerbockers were descendants of early Dutch settlers in New York and are a New York basketball team.)

340. Red Top Brewing Company of Cincinnati, Ohio.

341. Glueks from Gluek Brewing Company.

342. Free State Brewery of Baltimore, Maryland.

343. Croft Brewing Company. Croft labels depicted three men drinking beer with the caption: "Dry, Pure, and Sparkling."

344. Chester Brewery of Chester.

345. Chartiers Valley Brewery of Carnegie, Pennsylvania. This brewery was owned by the Duquesne Brewing Company of Pittsburgh.

346. Ph. Schneider Brewing Company of Trinidad, Colorado, for Century Beer.

347. Altes Lager from Tivoli Brewing Company. In 1948 Tivoli became Altes Brewing Company and in 1954 became National Brewing Company. It closed in 1973.

348. Washington Brewing Company of Washington, Pennsylvania. The brewery operated from 1933–1940.

349. Kessler from Kessler Brewing Company of Helena, Montana. This early Montana brewery was founded by Charles Beehrer in 1864. Kessler became a partner in 1865 and took control in 1866. It was renamed Kessler Brewing Company in 1900 and survived until 1958 with a sixteen-year rest during Prohibition.

350. Jung from Jung Brewing Company of Milwaukee, Wisconsin.

351. Diehl Brewing Company of Defiance, Ohio.

352. Pickwick Beer.

353. Centennial Brewing Company. This Butte, Montana, brewery closed in 1918 at Prohibition.

354. Gilt Top. (Spokane, Washington).

355. The home. One Doelger Ale can reads, "A priceless difference in flavor."

356. Fred Krug Brewing Company. Krug was one of the first brewers to fall to large company takeovers when Falstaff of St. Louis expanded in 1935.

357. Wisconsin Lager. The brewer was Potosi Brewing Company.

358. Belmont from Martins Ferry, Ohio.

359. Northern Brewing Company of Superior, Wisconsin, for Northern Beer.

360. Tivoli. From Denver, Colorado, Tivoli also played on the backward spelling of its name in advertising. Read it backward!

361. Progress. It was made by Progress Brewing Company of Oklahoma City, which was only one of six brewers ever to operate in Oklahoma. Progress Brewing Company was formed after Prohibition and was purchased in 1960 by Lone Star Brewing Company of San Antonio, Texas, which operated it until 1971.

362. Muehlebach Brewing Company. The brewery was founded by John Hurt in 1864. The Muehlebach family purchased the brewery in 1870. It remained in the family until 1956 when it was sold to Schlitz of Milwaukee. Schlitz closed the brewery in 1973.

363. G. Weber Brewing Company of Theresa, Wisconsin. The brewery was founded by Benedict Weber and survived over one hundred years until 1961.

364. Chr. Heurich Brewing Company of Washington, D.C. The brewery was actually founded in 1864 by George Schnell. Heurich joined the operation in 1872 as a partner of Paul Ritter. Heurich took over ownership in 1873.

365. Deer Park Breweries. The brewery operated prior to Prohibition from 1899–1922. After Prohibition it was open from 1933 to 1942.

366. Schmidts from Jacob Schmidt Brewing Company. Schmidts is now owned by G. Heileman Brewing Company of LaCrosse, Wisconsin.

367. Schultz. From Union City, New Jersey, Schultz operated from 1934–1938.

368. Pabst. The brewery was founded in 1844 by Jacob Best. In March, 1984, California investor Paul Kalmanovitz took control of this Milwaukee-based brewer and was fighting takeover attempts from the G. Heileman Brewing Company of LaCrosse, Wisconsin.

369. Blatz. This brewery was used for the production of industrial alcohol during Prohibition.

370. Peter Doelger Brewing Company. In the thirties, Doelger operated breweries in Brooklyn, Kingston, and New York, New York; and in Newark, New Jersey. The Newark operation was the most successful and survived under Doelger until 1948.

371. From 1874 to Prohibition, Utah had forty breweries operating, but only two survived Prohibition. Becker was founded in 1894 and closed in 1965. General Brewing, Utah's last brewery, closed two years later.

372. Imperial Beer from Erie Brewing Company. Erie went out of business in 1978 after 123 years of operation.

373. Schlitz. The Schlitz brand is now owned by the Stroh Brewery of Detroit. The slogan was introduced in 1872. The brewery had shipped beer to Chicago after the 1871 fire. Subsequently, sales shot up fifty percent and Schlitz became the beer that "Made Milwaukee Famous."

374. Rahr. The brewery was located in both Green Bay and Oshkosh, Wisconsin.

375. Silitel. Brewed by the Wilber Brewery Company of Wilber, Nebraska, Wilber was a small turn-of-the-century brewery that closed in 1917.

376. Olympia Brewing Company. Olympia is located in the Tumwater suburb of Olympia. It was purchased by Pabst Brewing Company of Milwaukee in 1983.

377. The Salem Brewery Association. Salem operated in Salem, Oregon from 1903–1916 and 1934–1943.

378. Aberdeen Brewing Company. Aberdeen was in business from 1901–1915.

379. Walla Walla Brewing Company. The brewery was located in Walla Walla, Washington from 1914–1926.

380. P. O. C. Brewed by the Pilsener Brewing Company, P. O. C. is an abbreviation for Pride of Cleveland.

381. Elfenbrau. The beer was brewed by the C. & J. Michel Brewing Company, which operated from 1882–1920.

382. Reisch Beer. Brewed by the Reisch Brewing Company, which was founded by Frank Reisch in 1849. The name continued through 1966.

383. Park Brewing Company. Park operated at the corner of Front and Walnut streets in Winona, Minnesota, from 1905–1920.

384. Becker Products Company. Becker was located in Ogden, Utah. Becker was a cereal beverage.

385. Dubuque Brewing & Malting Company. The brewery was in Dubuque, Iowa.

386. Joliet Citizens Brewing Company.

387. "Opens the way to health." The brewery was located in St. Charles, Missouri.

388. Southern Select was advertised this way prior to Prohibition. After Prohibition this brand name was purchased by the Galveston-Houston Brewing Company of Galveston.

389. Feigenspan. It was made by Christian Feigenspan Brewing Company of Newark.

390. Acme. Brewed by the Acme brewing company of San Francisco.

391. Kulminator. From Kulmbach, Germany, Kulminator has a 13.2 percent alcohol.

392. Wisconsin. Eau Claire, Wisconsin, has one bar for every 629 people, which is the highest concentration in the United States. Wisconsin, however, trailed New Hampshire in 1984 in twelve ounce bottles of beer consumed per capita (498 versus 559). Lowest consumption in 1984 was Tennessee, with 285 bottles per capita.

393. Generally 3.7 percent by weight and 4.6 percent by volume.

394. 3.2 percent. (Purchaser must be at least eighteen years old).

395. They both contain 150 calories.

396. F. X. Matt Brewing Company (formerly West End Brewing Company). This independent brewery is still operating at 811 Edward Street, Utica, New York.

397. Buckeye Brewing Company. Buckeye was located in Toledo, Ohio, until 1966, when it was purchased by Meister Brau of Chicago. Meister Brau closed the brewery in 1972.

398. Rheingold, at its Forrest Brewing Company branch in New Bedford, Massachusetts, in 1968. The brand was Gablinger's and the label read "Has only 99 calories—⅓ less than our regular beers."

399. Generally, a glass of beer drunk with a shot of either liqueur or whiskey, depending upon the area of the country in which it is ordered.

400. Storz Brewing Company of Omaha, Nebraska, brewed the beer Storz-ette from 1961–1965.

401. Champagne Velvet. It was brewed by the Terre Haute Brewing Company from 1935–1958.

402. Felsenbrau from Clyffside Brewing Company. The brewery was located on McMicken Avenue and produced Felsenbrau until it was purchased by the Red Top Brewing Company in 1945.

403. The brand name was used at the Greensburg Brewing Company from 1933–1935. The brewery became Victor Brewing Company in 1936 and when it was changed to Old Reliable Brewing Company in 1941, the brand was adopted again.

404. Genesee. From Rochester, New York, Genesee is still operating and has a capacity of four million barrels per year. It was the seventh largest brewery in the United States in 1984.

405. Fort Pitt. Fort Pitt was brewed by Fort Pitt Brewing Company of Pennsylvania from 1933–1958.

406. Braumeister. Braumeister was made by Independent Milwaukee Brewery of Milwaukee, Wisconsin from 1933–1964.

407. Mausner. It was made from 1933–1936.

408. Old Mission Lager. Old Mission was a pre-Prohibition brand.

409. Pabst Blue Ribbon.

410. Brackenridge Brewing Company. From Brackenridge, Pennsylvania, the brewery operated from 1933–1941.

411. Peter Hand Brewing Company. Hand produced Old Chicago Beer from 1973–1978.

412. Old German Beer.

413. Old Gold. Also Miller Brewing Company, after the 1970 takeover by Philip Morris, produced Marlboro Beer; it lasted only two years.

414. Fountain City Brewing Company. The brewery, located in Fountain City, Wisconsin, operated from 1933–1935.

415. Old Dutch from Old Dutch Brewers. Several other brewers used the Old Dutch brand name, including Maier of Los Angeles; Old Dutch of Detroit; International Breweries of Findlay, Ohio; and Neuweiler of Allentown, Pennsylvania.

416. Peter Hand Brewing Company.

417. Atlas Prager from Atlas Brewing Company.

418. Burger Brewing Company. Located in Cincinnati, Ohio, Burger sponsored the Cincinnati Reds' baseball games on radio from the early 1940s until 1967.

419. Meister Brau from Peter Hand Brewing Company. Meister Brau is well-known for a number of beer can sets, including Fiesta Pack of the 1950s, the Winter Carnival of 1953, and the Happy Days Toasts of 1957.

420. Regal from Regal Brewing Company, San Francisco, California. What beer the ad agency had in mind for the other of the two is unknown. Note what *Regal* is spelled backward!

421. Coors of Golden, Colorado.

422. Storz Brewing Company of Omaha. This brewer was purchased by Grain Belt Breweries of Minneapolis in 1967 and closed in 1972.

423. Lucky Lager from Lucky Lager Brewing Company in San Francisco, California.

424. Von Beer from Von Brewing Company.

425. Ebling's Extra. The brewer was Ebling Brewing Company, which operated from 1868–1950.

426. Flock Brewing Company of Williamsport, Pennsylvania. Flock was one of the earliest breweries in central Pennsylvania, started in 1854 by Jacob Hoffman.

427. Hyde Park. It was brewed by Hyde Park Brewery from 1933–1954.

428. Blatz' Private Stock. The Blatz brewery was founded in 1851 by Valentine Blatz at the corner of Broadway and Division.

429. Gold Bond from Cleveland-Sandusky Brewing Company from 1933–1962.

430. Grand Island Brewing Company of Grand Island, Nebraska, which operated from 1902–1917.

431. Falls City Lager, Louisville, Kentucky.

432. Geo. Walter Brewing Company of Appleton, Wisconsin.

433. Jackson Brewing Company for Jax Beer from 1933 to 1974. The Jackson Brewery was reopened as a shopping center in 1984 after extensive renovations.

434. Tacoma Brewing Company of San Francisco, California.

435. Schaefer Brewing Company. Schaefer closed its Brooklyn plant in 1976. It was the last surviving Brooklyn brewery. Schaefer is now brewed by the Stroh Brewery branch at Allentown, Pennsylvania (formerly the Schaefer brewery).

436. Riverview Brewing Company. Located in Manitowoc, Wisconsin. Riverview was a short lived brewery only operating from 1933–1937.

437. Majestic from Independent Brewing Company.

438. Hack & Simon of Vincennes, Indiana. This brewery closed in 1918 and an attempt was made in 1934 to reopen it as the Old Vincennes Brewery. It never reopened.

439. Hocking Valley Brewing Company. The brewery operated from 1905–1919 and 1948–1950.

440. Eastside. It was brewed by the Los Angeles Brewing Company in California.

441. Calumet Brewing Company. The brewery was located in Chilton, Wisconsin, and produced Badger Brew from 1939–1942. The brand name was also used by Effinger Brewing (Baraboo), Reedsburg Brewery (Reedsburg), and Oshkosh Brewing (Oshkosh).

442. Ruhstallers. It was brewed by the Buffalo Brewing Company, which operated from 1933–1942.

443. Sioux City Brewing Company. It was located in Sioux City, Iowa.

444. Moerlein Brewing Company. Moerlein was in Cincinnati, Ohio, prior to Prohibition (closed 1919). Since Prohibition, the Red Top Brewing Company of Cincinnati, the Associated Brewery of South Bend, Indiana and the Terre Haute Brewing Company of Terre Haute, Indiana, have all used the Barbarossa brand name.

445. Los Angeles Brewing Company. This brewery was founded in 1897, sold out to Pabst of Milwaukee in 1953, and closed in 1979.

446. Triumph Beer and Old Saxon Brau from Storz Brewing Company. Both brands were brewed prior to Prohibition. The Triumph name was resurrected from 1952–1958; and the Old Saxon name from 1933–1939.

447. John Graf Company of Milwaukee, Wisconsin. Graf operated from 1874–1920.

448. Stanton Brewery of Troy, New York. Founded by Stanton in 1874, the brewery survived until 1950.

449. Duquesne Pilsener from Duquesne Brewing Company of Pittsburgh, Pennsylvania. Another Duquesne brand, Duke, was labeled "The Prince of Pilseners."

450. Gambrinus Lager from Gambrinus Brewing Company. It was produced from 1933–1935.

451. Buckeye Brewing Company. Buckeye was located in Toledo, Ohio. Kraeusening is a process of adding young beer to fully aged beer to introduce a natural increase in carbon dioxide.

452. Blatz. (A strange claim is made on an early Blatz beer *can*—"Milwaukee's First Bottled Beer!" On a can?)

453. Narragansett Brewing Company. Narragansett was purchased by national brewer Falstaff in 1965.

454. Carling's Black Label. Black Label cans carry the statement "The World's leading internationally brewed beer."

455. Gambrinus from August Wagner Breweries of Columbus, Ohio.

456. Pabst Brewing Company. The answer is Pabst Blue Ribbon.

457. Hensler. It was brewed by the Joseph Hensler Brewing Company of Newark, New Jersey, from 1935–1958.

458. Schmidt Brewing Company. Schmidt's is still producing beer at 127 Edward Street.

459. Washington Beer. Washington Breweries was located in Columbus, Ohio from 1906–1953.

460. Pablo. This was a near beer.

461. Iron City from Pittsburgh. Iron City is still brewed by the Pittsburgh Brewing Company on Liberty Avenue.

462. Edelweiss. It was produced by Schoenhofen-Edelweiss Company of Chicago, Illinois.

463. Blumer Brewing Corporation of Monroe, Wisconsin. Since 1947 this brewery has been the Joseph Huber Brewing Company, which has gained some national fame through its Augsburger Beer.

464. Harry Mitchell Brewing Company of El Paso, Texas. Mitchell was the only brewer in El Paso. It was founded in 1905 as the El Paso Brewing Association. After Prohibition, it was reopened by Harry Mitchell and was sold in 1955 to Falstaff of St. Louis. It closed in 1967.

465. Supreme. It was brewed from 1933–1955.

466. Glennons. The Pittston Brewing Company of Pittston, Pennsylvania, brewed Glennons and operated from 1934–1942.

467. Emmerling from Emmerling Brewing Company. The brewery was founded by John Emmerling in 1878 and went out of business in 1920.

468. Andeker. Introduced in 1939, Andeker was the Pabst Brewing Company's premium brand.

469. (Jacob) Hornung Brewing Company's.

470. Indianapolis Brewing Company of Indianapolis, Indiana.

471. Walter Brewing Company in Eau Clarie. Walter is a small, independent brewery. It is still operating, with a production capacity of 150,000 barrels of beer per year.

472. Hanley's Peerless Ale from the James Hanley Brewing Company of Providence, Rhode Island.

473. Arrow Beer from Kamm & Schellinger of Mishawaka, Indiana; and Globe Brewing Company of Balitmore. A similar slogan, "Hits the spot," was used by Peoples Beer from Peoples Brewing Company of Duluth, Minnesota.

474. Jones Brewing Company in Smithton, Pennsylvania. This small brewery (150,000 barrels of beer per year) currently brews Stoney's Gold Crown, Esquire, Fort Pitt, and Old Shay brands.

475. Moose Beer from Moose Brewing Company of Roscoe, Pennsylvania, which operated from 1933–1949.

476. Schmidt. Jacob Schmidt Brewing Company was located in St. Paul, Minnesota.

477. Atlantic Beer. Atlantic was brewed by several southern breweries in Orlando, Florida; Atlanta, Georgia; Charlotte, North Carolina; Chattanooga, Tennessee; and Norfolk, Virginia.

478. Pfeiffer. Pfeiffer Brewing Company was located in Detroit, Michigan from 1890 to 1962.

479. Chief Oshkosh. Oshkosh Brewing Company was located in Oshkosh, Wisconsin. Oshkosh went out of business in 1971.

480. National. National Brewing Company was located in Baltimore, Maryland. National merged with Carling Brewing Company in 1975 and their operations were sold to G. Heileman of Wisconsin in 1979.

481. Leinenkugel. It is still brewed in Chippewa Falls, Wisconsin by the Jacob Leinenkugel Brewing Company, which was founded in 1867.

482. Fox Head 400 beer. Fox Head Brewing Company was located in Waukesha, Wisconsin from 1946–1962.

483. Altes from Altes Brewing Company. Located in San Diego, California, Altes was a branch of Altes in Detroit from 1949–1953.

484. A-1 from the Arizona Brewing Company of Phoenix, Arizona. This brewery became part of the Carling National merger in 1975 and was sold to G. Heileman Brewing of LaCrosse, Wisconsin, in 1979. It is still in operation.

485. Burger Brewing Company of Cincinnati, Ohio.

486. Charles D. Kaier Company of Mahanoy City for its Old Diamond Ale and Porter. Kaier was founded in 1880 and closed in 1968.

487. Kalamazoo Brewing Company of Kalamazoo, Michigan from 1904–1915.

488. West End Brewing Company of Utica, New York.

489. Phoenix Beer of Buffalo, New York.

490. Metz from Metz Brewing Company of Omaha, Nebraska.

491. Berkshire Brewing Association of Pittsfield, Massachusetts from 1891–1918.

492. Gold Nugget from Black Hills Brewing Company of Central City, South Dakota.

493. Cataract Beer from the Cataract Brewing Company of Rochester, New York. Cataract was brewed from 1933–1940.

494. Burkhardt. The Burkhardt Brewing Company of Akron, Ohio, brewed Burkhardt from 1934–1957.

495. Hamm's from Theodore Hamm Brewing Company of St. Paul, Minnesota. Hamm's is now owned by the Stroh Brewery of Detroit.

496. Feigenspan. The Christian Feigenspan Brewing Company was located in Newark.

497. Hudepohl Beer from Hudepohl Brewing Company. 1985 was the hundredth anniversary celebration for this brewery.

498. Pearl. The Pearl Brewing Company of San Antonio is still going strong at 312 Pearl Parkway.

499. Coors of Golden, Colorado. In 1984 Coors was the fifth largest beer producer in the United States. All beer was brewed in a single plant.

500. Schoenling. This brewery is still in operation at 1625 Central Parkway.